Health Matters
Drugs and Your Health

by Jillian Powell

RAINTREE
STECK-VAUGHN
PUBLISHERS
The Steck-Vaughn Company

Austin, Texas

Titles in the series

Drugs and Your Health
Exercise and Your Health
Food and Your Health
Hygiene and Your Health

Published by Raintree Steck-Vaughn Publishers,
an imprint of Steck-Vaughn Company

Library of Congress Cataloging-in-Publication Data
Powell, Jillian.
Drugs and Your Health / Jillian Powell.
     p.   cm.—(Health Matters)
     Includes bibliographical references and index.
     Summary: Discusses drug benefits and problems
     and how to become more knowledgeable about each.
     ISBN 0-8172-4928-1
     1. Drugs—Physiological effect—Juvenile literature.
     2. Drug abuse—Juvenile literature.
     [1. Drugs. 2. Drug abuse.]
     I. Title. II. Series: Health matters.
     RM301.17.P69 1998
     615'.1—dc21   97-19064

Printed in Italy. Bound in the United States.
1 2 3 4 5 6 7 8 9 0 02 01 00 99 98

Picture acknowledgments
Allsport 21(top); Format 23 (top right); Sally & Richard Greenhill Photo Library 14; The Hutchison Library 28; Popperfoto 22 (bottom left); Science Photo Library 8 (both), 23 (center left & right); South American Pictures 12; Tony Stone 4, 6, 7, 11, 15, 22 (right), 24, 26; Topham 13; Wayland Picture Library 9; Zefa Picture Library 10, 16, 19, 20, 21 (bottom), 23 (top left).

Contents

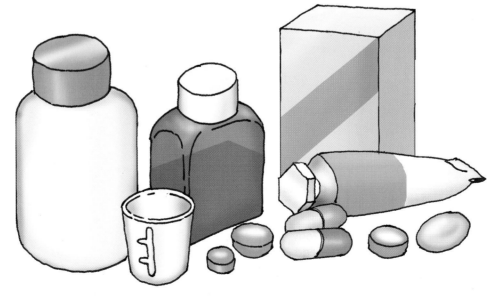

What Are Drugs?

Drugs are substances that change the way our bodies and minds work. Some drugs help the body repair itself while others can prevent illness or disease. Drugs from the doctor can be used to help your body get back to normal health. However, if they are not used properly or if they are used for the wrong reasons, some drugs stop being helpful and become dangerous. Some drugs can block the action of natural chemicals in the body.

Tobacco, alcohol, and illegal drugs can be harmful to your body and mind. They can cause fatal diseases and even death.

Medicines help make you feel better and get your energy back. Although they may make you feel good at first, illegal drugs can make you sick and cause bad feelings.

Right: There are hundreds of different types of drugs. They come as tablets, capsules, liquids, or creams. Some can be inhaled or injected.

Some drugs are more powerful than others. The effect that a drug has on your body depends on your age, size, and health.

Right: Tea, coffee, and soda may all contain the drug caffeine. Caffeine is an addictive drug. If you drink eight cups of coffee a day (.017 to .021 oz. [500 to 600 mg] of caffeine) your body will get used to caffeine. When you stop drinking it, you may have headaches and feel grumpy and jittery and even sick.

Drugs That Make You Better

Drugs that make illness or pain better are called medicines. They include painkillers, cough and cold medicines, diarrhea and stomach settlers, and antihistamines for allergies such as hay fever. Antibiotics are drugs that fight infections by killing bacteria in the body.

Some medicines can be bought "over the counter" from drugstores and supermarkets. Others have to be prescribed by a doctor.

The doctor figures out which drug and how much the patient needs. Then she checks the details on a computer. The doctor gives the patient a prescription. The patient then takes the prescription to a drugstore to get it filled.

Right: The body has its own immune system for fighting germs and illnesses. Viruses such as colds and some stomach upsets can often be cured simply by resting and drinking lots of liquids.

Left: There is no cure for colds and flu, but there are medicines that can help you feel more comfortable. Find out from a pharmacist which drugs they contain and how they work.

Living Longer

As a result of modern medicines, people can expect to live twice as long as they used to hundreds of years ago. As more people live on into their eighties, they may suffer from diseases such as arthritis or heart disease. Drugs can help them stay alive and live more comfortably.

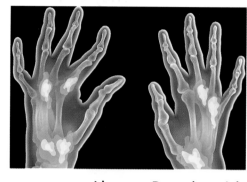

Above: People with swollen joints caused by arthritis are given drugs that block the chemicals that cause pain.

People with high blood pressure are given drugs. These drugs block a chemical that makes the blood vessels tighter, which means the blood can flow more easily.

Some people need to take drugs all their lives to help them live normally. People with diabetes don't have enough of a chemical named insulin, which the body needs to break down and use as sugar. They have to inject themselves every day with insulin that is made by scientists in a laboratory.

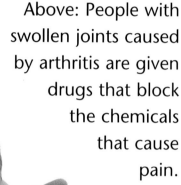

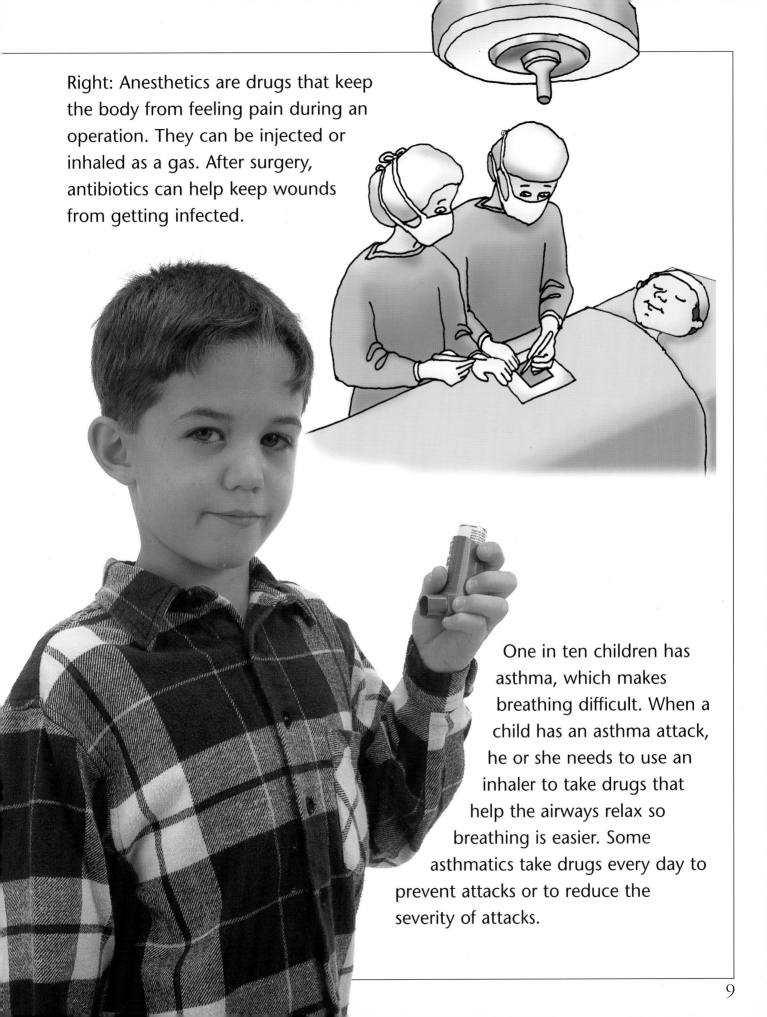

Right: Anesthetics are drugs that keep the body from feeling pain during an operation. They can be injected or inhaled as a gas. After surgery, antibiotics can help keep wounds from getting infected.

One in ten children has asthma, which makes breathing difficult. When a child has an asthma attack, he or she needs to use an inhaler to take drugs that help the airways relax so breathing is easier. Some asthmatics take drugs every day to prevent attacks or to reduce the severity of attacks.

9

How Drugs Are Made

Drugs are made in laboratories from chemicals that are either made by humans or taken from plants or animals. It can take years to find and test a new drug.

Scientists look for drugs that will match natural chemicals in the body. They start by designing chemical models on a computer screen, then make up the drugs in the laboratory and begin tests. Tests may be carried out on dead animal flesh and then on live laboratory animals such as mice or rats.

Scientists are always looking for new drugs to cure diseases such as cancer, multiple sclerosis, and HIV.

Some people feel that animals should not be used to test drugs designed for human use. But many scientists feel that it is better to test a drug that may be dangerous on animals before it is given to humans.

If these tests are successful, the drug is given to groups of human volunteers to make sure that it is safe to be given to patients.

Right: Plants have been used as medicines for thousands of years. Many modern drugs contain plant extracts. Digitalis, from foxglove leaves, is used in drugs for heart disease. Opium from poppies is used to make painkillers such as morphine.

Find out about as many medicines and drugs as you can that come from plants. Visit a health store and look in magazines for advertisements for drugs that use plant extracts.

Drugs in the Past

People have been using drugs for thousands of years, for medicine or relaxation or during religious ceremonies and celebrations.

The peoples of the Andes in South America chewed coca leaves, which contain cocaine, to boost their energy. And opium and cannabis were widely used in Asia to kill pain and bring relaxation. Tobacco was smoked by Amerindian tribes, and the Aztecs of Mexico used magic mushrooms. These made them feel strange and see things that weren't actually happening during their religious ceremonies.

A woman sells coca leaves to a Quecha Indian at a market in the highlands of Peru. When the dried leaves are chewed, it makes people feel excited and boosts their energy.

Right: In the 1920s, alcohol was banned in the United States by a law known as Prohibition. This led to the illegal making and smuggling of alcohol until the law ended in 1933.

Left: Some pilots during World War II took amphetamines to keep them awake.

Right: In the 1950s and 1960s, cannabis and LSD (acid) were popular drugs for young people involved in the Flower Power Movement.

How Drugs Work

Drugs come in many forms. Some can be injected into the blood or inhaled so that they start to work immediately. Others need to work more slowly and gradually. Tiny particles are coated in capsules that release them in stages.

Our body cells have special pieces called receptors that receive the chemicals. They have a particular shape. When matching chemicals reach them, the receptors join in the same way as jigsaw pieces. Drugs can copy natural chemicals in the body or keep them from working.

It is important to measure the right amount of medicine into the measuring spoon.

Syringes work like bicycle pumps, using air pressure to pump medicine through the fine metal tube of the needle into the bloodstream.

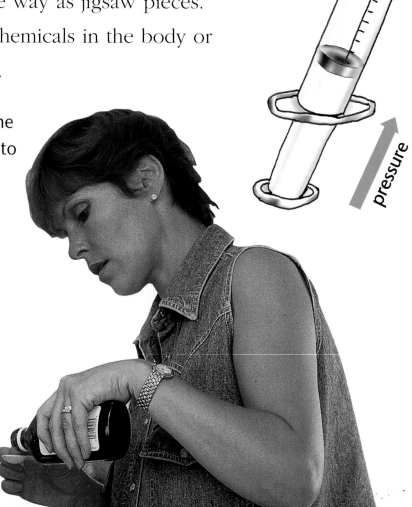

pressure

Blood carries drugs to the body cells that need them.

Some drugs are broken down in the liver, and only a small amount gets into the blood.

Some drugs have to be injected because stomach juices would destroy them.

Drugs that are not needed pass through the kidneys and out of the body in urine.

Body size affects how a drug works.

Drugs taken by mouth begin to break down in the stomach. Food helps some drugs work more quickly.

Liver

Stomach

Kidney

Intestines

Drugs taken by mouth travel via the stomach and intestine before passing into the bloodstream.

Some medicines are made specially for children. Find out about as many children's medicines as you can. In what ways are they different from adults' medicines?

Safety and Drugs

All drugs can be harmful if they are not used properly. Labels carry important safety information. They give the correct dosage, measured in milligrams (mgs) for tablets and milliliters (mls) for liquids. They tell the patient how often to take the drug and whether to take it before, with, or after, food.

Some drugs must not be taken with alcohol or certain foods such as milk, which can keep antibiotics from working properly. Labels warn of side effects such as drowsiness or that patients should not use machinery while they are taking certain drugs.

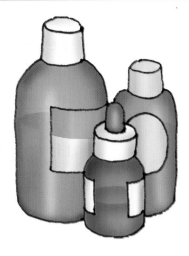

Above: Drugs must be stored in a cool, dark place because light and heat can spoil them. Dark blue or brown glass or plastic keeps out sunlight. Most medicines have a "use by" date.

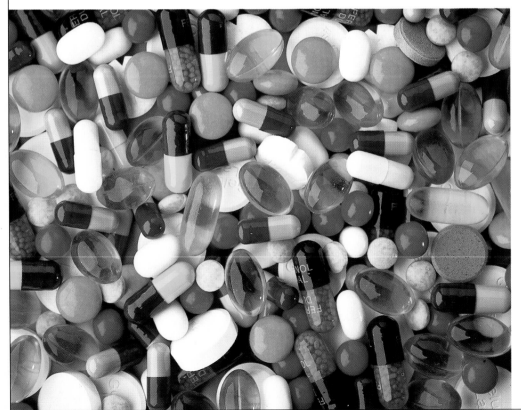

Left: Colorful tablets and capsules can look like candies to small children. They should be kept out of reach in a medicine cabinet. Special caps keep children from being able to open bottles and jars.

It is important never to take someone else's medicine even if you think you have the same illness. It could be dangerous and is against the law.

Imagine that you have to put together the contents of a new medicine and first-aid cabinet for your school. What would you include and why? What safety measures would you take to keep drugs safe?

Drinking and Smoking

In many countries, tobacco and alcohol are the most commonly used legal drugs. People use them to feel more lively or relaxed, but both are addictive drugs that can harm the body. More people die from heart and lung diseases because of the nicotine in tobacco smoke than from any other drug.

Right: If a woman is pregnant, alcohol or tobacco can harm or even kill her unborn baby.

Below: Passive smoking means breathing in other people's smoke. Fifteen percent is breathed in by the smoker while the rest goes into the surrounding air.

Many adults and teenagers drink alcohol. In fact, drinking a small amount of alcohol can be good for people. Although there are safe amounts of alcohol that can be drunk, too much of it can kill people by damaging their livers. Alcohol abuse is also the cause of many road accidents and violent crimes.

Alcohol can destroy vitamins in food and damage the lining of the stomach.

Smoke wrinkles and ages the skin.

Smoking causes yellow teeth, bad breath, and stops food tasting good.

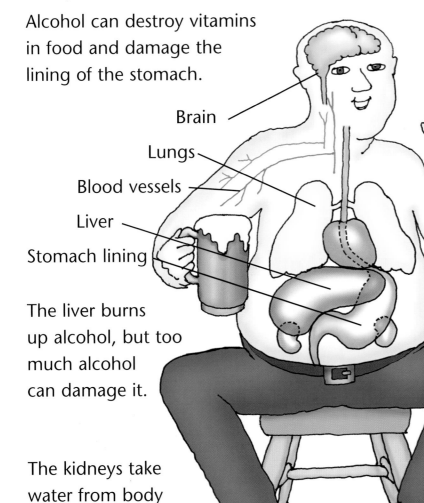

Brain

Lungs

Blood vessels

Liver

Stomach lining

The liver burns up alcohol, but too much alcohol can damage it.

Tar from tobacco smoke clogs the lungs and contains chemicals that cause cancer.

Carbon monoxide is a poisonous gas in tobacco smoke that can keep blood from carrying enough oxygen to the brain and muscles.

Nicotine makes blood vessels tighter and blood more sticky, so it flows less easily around the body.

The kidneys take water from body cells to flush out alcohol in urine. This causes dehydration.

Drugs in Sports

Some sportspeople use drugs to build muscles, give them energy, calm their nerves, or hide pain. Some of the drugs they take can be used legally as medicine but are banned from sports. Others are illegal drugs.

When drugs are taken, they pass into the blood and then out of the body in urine. Sports authorities take urine samples from sportsplayers before and after major sports events. If drugs are found in their urine, they may be banned from sports for months, years, or sometimes forever.

Some sportspeople take drugs to try and help them win. Others believe taking drugs is cheating and campaign against drug use in sports.

Above: Some athletes take illegal drugs such as cocaine and amphetamines to make them more energetic and competitive. They are addictive drugs and have side effects, including high blood pressure and heart rate.

Below: Anabolic steroids act like male hormones and build muscle. They are taken as tablets or injected into the muscles. They are legal as medicine but banned from sports. They can have dangerous side effects such as heart disease, liver cancer, and mood changes.

Below: Beta-blockers are used to slow the heart rate and calm nerves. Doctors can prescribe them legally, but they can cause heart and breathing problems if misused.

Left: Athletes sometimes need to take drugs for injuries. Painkillers may let an athlete continue even after injury.

Illegal Drugs

Drugs that some people use illegally are the kind that go to the brain to make strange feelings happen. They can make people feel excited and happy, relaxed and sleepy, or dizzy and strange. Some illegal drugs can make people see things that are not actually there.

Below: Nine illegal drugs— (left to right): heroin, Ecstacy, cannabis leaves (top row), magic mushrooms, acid (LSD), cannabis resin (center row), cocaine, crack, and speed (bottom row).

Some drugs can also make you feel bad about yourself and harm your body and mind. Many people who use them start to need more, because they spend more time feeling bad and less time feeling good.

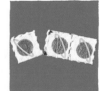

Some people take Ecstasy (E) in clubs to give them more energy. It can cause overheating known as heatstroke. Some people have even died from taking it.

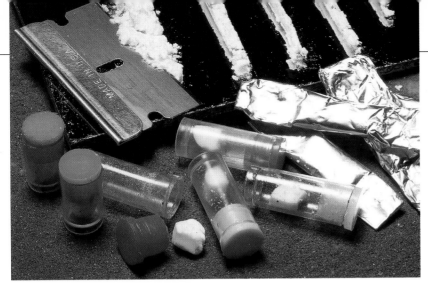

Above: Cocaine is injected or sniffed. A similar drug named crack is smoked or sniffed. These drugs speed up heart rate and give energy, but they are addictive and can cause panic and terrible anxiety.

Amphetamines boost energy but can cause panic, eating and sleeping problems and may damage blood vessels.

Right: LSD (acid) is a hallucinogenic drug that makes people feel strange and see odd pictures in their heads. Such drugs can cause fear, panic, and strange behavior.

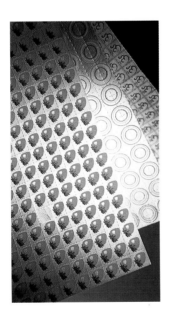

Left: Smoking cannabis makes people feel relaxed, but it can cause lung cancer and make people think less clearly. It has been linked with anxiety and sad feelings.

Solvents are everyday products, such as glue, aerosol sprays, lighter fluid, and nail polish, that give off a strong gas or fumes. Some people sniff or spray them into their mouths to feel excited or strange. They contain powerful chemicals that harm your body and could kill you.

Addictive Drugs

Drug addiction is the result of the mind and body needing a drug. Addictive drugs include alcohol, nicotine, tranquilizers, cocaine, and heroin. They cause chemical changes in the body that make it need more of the drug.

Often, drug addicts can't think of anything else except getting more drugs. For a while, the drug makes them feel better. But when they stop using it, they get sick with pain and anxiety. Many crimes, such as stealing and shoplifting, are carried out by some drug addicts who take drugs such as cocaine and heroin. They are desperate to get more money to buy these expensive drugs.

Babies whose mothers are drug addicts may be born addicted to the same drugs.

The effects on the body of taking Ecstacy.

Chemicals are released in the brain

Blemishes may appear on the skin.

Ecstasy can cause heatstroke and may damage the liver and brain cells. New research has proved that Ecstasy can cause depression years after it has been taken.

Kidney damage

Liver damage

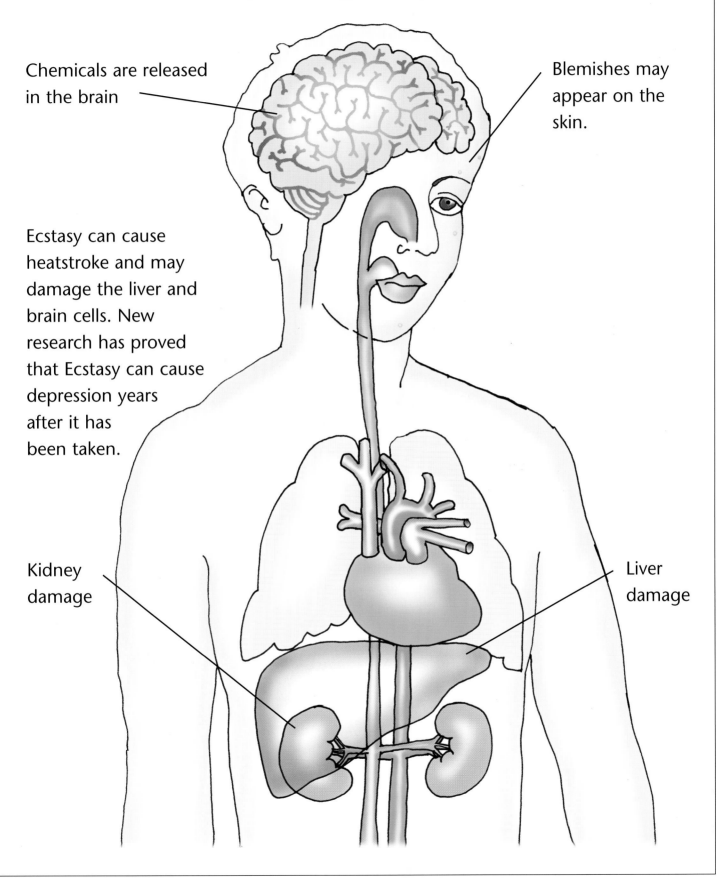

Problems with Drugs

Illegal drugs are a growing problem. Drug dealers make lots of money by selling them and often sell drugs so that they can afford drugs for themselves. People are constantly getting sick and dying from taking illegal drugs. Dealers are sometimes caught and sent to prison. Drugs coming into a country are sometimes found by the police before they reach the dealers.

A customs officer takes a sniffer dog on an airplane to make sure that there are no drugs hidden there.

Most countries have laws about drugs. In Great Britain, the United States, and Australia, possessing or selling drugs such as cocaine or heroin is illegal. It is also against the law to take any legal medicines that have been prescribed for somebody else.

In some Muslim countries, alcohol is illegal. Customs officers at ports and airports try to stop people from bringing illegal drugs into their countries. They use specially trained sniffer dogs to help them find hidden supplies of drugs.

Illegal drugs do not have safety checks as legal drugs do. They may be mixed with flour, talcum powder, chalk dust, or even poisonous substances. Sometimes tablets sold as drugs have been found to be other substances such as dog worming pills.

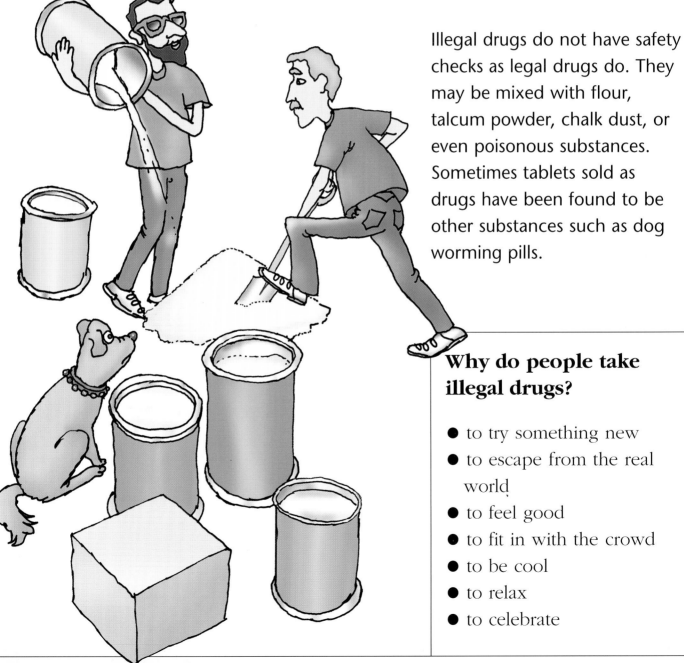

Why do people take illegal drugs?

- to try something new
- to escape from the real world
- to feel good
- to fit in with the crowd
- to be cool
- to relax
- to celebrate

The Good and the Bad

It is important to remember that prescribed drugs are there to make you feel better. These drugs are carefully tested in laboratories before they are given to people. If it were not for the many medicines available, there would be illnesses that could not be cured. Also, returning to full health after an illness would take much longer.

But illegal drugs can make you sick and can harm your body and mind. Any good feelings they give don't usually last for long. There are lots of other ways to feel good and to take care of your body.

Swimming and playing with your friends not only makes you feel good, but good exercise helps keep your body healthy.

Dancing, swimming, and running can make you feel good and happy. These activities produce natural chemicals in the body called endorphins. They go to your brain and make you feel good.

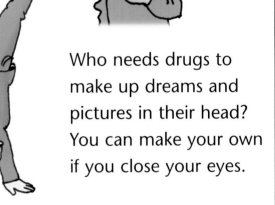

Cartwheels and somersaults can make you feel strange and dizzy.

Who needs drugs to make up dreams and pictures in their head? You can make your own if you close your eyes.

If someone tries to get you to taste or sniff a strange substance, you need to decide what is right and safe for you. Saying "no" may be harder than saying "yes," but learning to stand up for yourself is part of growing up.

Glossary

Addictive Something that you get used to and come to need.

Allergies Bad reactions to something.

Amphetamines Man-made chemicals that speed up heart rate and breathing and make you feel excited.

Anesthetics Substances given to patients so that they feel no pain.

Antihistamines Substances that reverse the effects of allergies.

Bacteria Tiny living things. Some are helpful but others can cause illness.

Caffeine A drug found in tea leaves and coffee beans that speeds up your heart rate.

Dehydration Lack of fluid in the body.

Dosage The correct amount of medicine to be taken each time.

Hallucinogenic A drug that causes strange pictures to form in the head.

HIV Human Immunodeficiency Virus —one of two viruses that causes AIDS.

Hormones Chemicals that are made in the body.

Immune system The body's own way of protecting itself from illness.

Intestine The long tube that runs from the stomach to the anus.

Multiple sclerosis An illness that causes paralysis and speech defects; it becomes gradually worse and has no cure.

Pharmacist The person at the drugstore who measures medicine from the doctor's prescription.

Prohibition A law that keeps people from making or selling alcohol.

Tranquilizers Drugs that are used to calm people; they are often used illegally.

Vaccines A weak form of disease injected to give protection against it.

Books to Read

Desmond, Theresa & Paul Almonte. *Drug Use and Abuse* (Update.) Parsippany, NJ: Silver Burdett Press, 1995.

DeStefano, Susan. *Focus on Medicines* (Drug Alert.) New York: 21st Century Books, 1991.

Edwards, Gabrielle. *Drugs on Your Street* (Drug Abuse Prevention Library.) New York: Rosen Group, 1993.

Hyde, Margaret O. *Know About Drugs, 4th Edition* (Know About.) New York: Walker and Co., 1995.

Nelson, Elizabeth. *Coping with Drugs and Sports* (Coping.) New York: Rosen Group, 1992.

Zeller, Paula K. *Focus on Marijuana* (Drug Alert.) New York: 21st Century Books, 1991.

Index

addictive 21, 23, 24-25
alcohol 4, 13, 16, 18-19, 24
anabolic steroids 21
anesthetics 9
animals 10, 11
antibiotics 6, 9, 16
arthritis 8

beta-blockers 21
blood 8, 14, 15, 18, 20, 21, 23
brain 18, 25

caffeine 5
crime 19, 24

dehydration 8
diabetes 8, 18
doctor 4, 6, 21
drug dealers 26
drugstore 6

Great Britain 26

heart 8, 11, 21, 23

illegal drugs 4, 20, 21, 24-8
  alcohol 27
  amphetamines 21, 23
  cannabis 12, 13, 23
  cocaine 12, 21, 23, 24, 26
  Ecstacy 4, 22, 25
  heroin 24, 26
  LSD 13, 23
  magic mushrooms 12, 22
  solvents 23
immune system 7

inhaled 5, 9, 14
injected 5, 8, 9, 14, 15, 21, 23

kidneys 15, 18, 25

laboratories 8, 10, 28
liver 15, 18, 19, 21, 25
lungs 18

medicine 6, 8, 11, 12, 15, 20, 26

opium 11, 12

painkillers 6, 11, 21
pharmacist 7
plants 10, 11
pregnancy 19
Prohibition 13

relaxation 12, 18

safety 16-17
scientists 8, 10, 11
side effects 16, 21
sports 20-21
stomach 6, 7, 15, 18
syringes 14

tobacco 4, 12, 18-19
  nicotine 18, 24

United States 13, 24
urine 15, 18, 20